You Are The Cloud

Mark Neill

For Rike

Acknowledgements:

The works of Rudolf Steiner,

    My teacher Else Klink.

With special thanks to Flurina, Noah and all in Scuol;

    And Judith whose idea it was,

and Genis, without whose help this book would not be what it is.

Copyright © Mark Neill 2023 ~ *All rights reserved.*

ISBN: 978-0-9873361-7-0

Published through Legion Office Works, Castlemaine.

Cover image: Rumpelstiltskin (photographer unknown).

Preface

A path to real progress – acting creatively, ethically, efficiently – requires freeing our breathing from imprisonment in the central nervous system.

Eurythmy, the art of visible speech, is this path. The body becoming a larynx releases our deepest impulses. A new Public Speaking in both word and deed is begun.

Based in the sounds (common to all languages) it will work in any place on Earth.

The alternative is the ever deeper descent into anxiety, asthma, disconnectedness, anger and violence.

In the normal run of things these sounds work together in an ever evolving creative, caring, supportive and harmonious interplay. Their abuse is also clear.

In a world become uncaring, stupid (in a stupor), greedy and gutless — where 'nothing works' and common sense an optional extra — harnessing the strength inherent in language may be the only way out.

Perhaps here lies the fulcrum where we can take control.

Contents

Extremes	6
You are the cloud	8
Eurythmy	10
The Social Art	18
Hidden Script	25
Engage	31
Fragmentation	34
The Sounds Have It!	37
Scarborough Fair	50
The Twelve Senses	65
Richard III	78
Chekov Acting Method	81
Two Tips	83
No Dreaming	88
It's All About	90
Believing	92
Simple Dwelling,	95

Hints, inklings, beginnings—

the rest over thousands of years.

Extremes
often show us the way.

A 20+ hour flight from Melbourne, Australia to Zurich, Switzerland knocks you out of yourself. You forget where you put your watch, your memory fails, you can't even talk properly.

Any surprise when you have been shot through the air at 800km/hr — stretched out over 16,000 km?

Any wonder you're not with it?

Even a short flight (say London to Vienna) is stressful, knocks us about a bit.

Hinders function.

We can't do our job so well.

But is everyday life any different? Are we not invaded by screens? Screens that suppress, as do money-worries, housing-worries, food-worries.

Poverty makes us anxious, physically ill.

And is too much money not sometimes also a problem?

Do we not often say I have too many things?

Do we act thereon?

Or remain burdened?

Too little or too much leads to anxiety, depression, even fear, hoarding, PTSD.

Will I kill myself?

Medication is often the only option.

Violence.

So much stops us from even finding what we want to do in life, let alone doing it.

    Why do we lack the courage to take the bull by the horns?

Where is the heart of the soldier? The limbs of the farmer?

    We go round and round in our nerves, internalizing not acting.

Our breathing gets caught-up, imprisoned in our central nervous system.

    We cannot breathe out.

And if you cannot breathe out you cannot breathe in.

    Perhaps here is the real cause of today's prevalence of asthma?

And is not cancer an illness about letting-go?

    ADHD an anxiety at not incarnating?

Are workplaces any different?

    We take it all home with us.

Complain and moan to family, close friends, not only work colleagues.

    Are we not stuck in our central nervous system?

Was not the original German expression for mental illness "Nervenkrankheit", illness of the nerves?

    Why do we pay small fortunes to go walking or biking in the Swiss Alps, to go to the gym?

Do we need to activate our bodies again?

    Do not activities chosen by many the world over not suggest this?

Do we sense disconnectedness?

You are the cloud

"Now is he winter of our discontent
Made glorious summer by this son of York,
And all the clouds that lowered upon our house
In the deep bosom of the ocean buried.
Now are our brows bound up with victorious wreathes,
Our bruised arms hung up for monuments
And now, instead of mounting barbed steeds…"

Shakespeare, in Richard III, would have it that we're a cloud, a deeply melancholic one.

    Is Hamlet not also so?

Macbeth,

    "So foul and fair day I have not seen."

But there are full-wispy, cirrus clouds – Sanguine ones.

    And watery ones. Laden with phlegma's heaviness.

Also lightening filled thunderous fireballs, full choler.

    All variations, combinations between.

Maybe a cloud is a good metaphor for the human condition?

    Clouds are continually changing shape.

Do we not also wish to be continually changing shape?

    Can the ability to be continually changing shape be learnt, developed, become permanent, second nature?

A habit?

Does not experience tell us everybody's a different cloud, becoming more so every day?

Sometimes from us as clouds great deeds of kindness but often great conflict, even nastiness, hate originate.

    From our words, deeds, body-language.
Can we find a way to take control and transform this unhappiness within?
    Having courage to speak what we're really trying to say.
Not killing with words, deeds, looks but bringing to life, birth?
    Can we happy if we're unable to express what's within?

Eurythmy
I

There is a language not thought-out ('abstract') that emerges from our words.

Eurythmy –

    The language of sounds.

Before every sound is a movement.

    Without the movement of the arm, the fist no banging on the door, no knock.

Before the sound *K* there is a *c*utting, chopping in, as the *k*ing or *c*on*qu*eror used to do.

    The discovery and initiation into the world of this artform in the first part last century allows making visible what is hidden in what is heard, expressing with our body what's within.

Anybody can do it.

    Do a '*k*arate' movement, chopping-in, brea*k*ing bric*k*s as *k*arate experts do!

Or a *B*.

    Em*b*racing someone.

An *L*, *l*ifting and fa*ll*ing *l*ike the waves.

As the actor trains his voice-body, so the eurythmist his physical body.

    The physical body becomes the instrument of expression.

A *L*arynx.

II

"*B*ring *m*e — At *o*nce — A *beer!*"

1. A curved inward movement with the right arm — holding it. *B*
2. Then a s*m*ooth movement of the right hand, palm facing inward, continues to the chest. *M*
3. A little hitting in with the fingers of the right hand, (held together) to the chest *T.*
4. A desce*n*ding movement of the right hand, palm facing downwards, followed by a quicker, more sudden lifting-up *N,*
    with *C* – lightness.
5. A closing of the left hand and its fingers round the handle of the glass.
6. A small, in 'indication' only, rolling movement with forearm and hand.
    (A small backwards — 'active' movement on Bring can be added.)

   Or

"*B*um" — a B movement curve with the bum.

"*N*o." A backwards curved movement of the right leg and foot, held with form at the end.

(Have you noticed how children saying 'no' scrunch-up their body a little to the right?)

Even our head can be a limb, expressive:

    Looking straight out horizontally says
        "I know".
    Dropping the head to chest
        "I know not".

Another example:

    "Parched,
    By the spirit's thirst,
    I crossed an endless desert
    Sunk in gloom…"
        (Pushkin).

1. When you're parched you're contained, in yourself and suffering — pain: to your body with both arms

2. But opening up with **A** upwards a bit, just as you write **A**, with your feelings/soul wanting water

3. 'by', staying close, **B**

4. To **SPR** spread out S of the snake seeking in the spirit Rolling out, 'unrolling'

5. A left to right movement of the whole body to another place, a karate chopping in movement **K**, rolling on with **R**
   D, staying anchored: you don't get that flippant crossing a desert on foot.
   Two more **D**'s, **d**own.

6. One sinking down movement where you stand, and ruminating (gloom) **U**, arms parallel with hands clasped together.

There is nothing mystical, mysterious here. Only a making visible of what lies hidden in the words, in the sounds.

Indeed, how we *WRiTe* each sound is a crystallization of the movement that brings that sound about through the movement of larynx, tongue, teeth, lips, etc. — with the breath moving through.

Eg. Opening your straightened arms, not too wide, gives *A*

- Picking up something we believe to be very heavy but turns out to be as light as air

    ⇨ *C*, movement of a pair of scales.

- The *S* movement of a snake speaks for itself.

Examining a diagram of a larynx reveals a little human being with wings, a Noh theatre practitioner from Japan. Lots of flexible ligament/muscle type material that <u>moves</u>.

> The Noh actor, Eurythmist traditionally has lots of material on that moves, shaped by the craft of the artist.

The eurythmist costumed mainly in silk projects colour best, moves best, beautifully.

> Eurythmy enables the body to become that little human being, that larynx … but full size.

Freeing the breathing from imprisonment in the central nervous system.

> Fear, anxiety, depression etc., becoming expression.

III

Of course, the professional eurythmist is challenged with making whole fairy tales visible.

Bringing to life Hamlet's soliloquies, works of great poets and writers, famous speeches (eg, The Testimony of Chief Seattle, indigenous stories, non-sense and comical verse).

Here we often work in groups.

Here not only the movement of the sounds in infinite variation, their moods as befitting the piece but movements for grammar, the meaning must be found, uncovered.

As the backwards movement by "Bring me" in the example above. It may also be a little bit curved — a <u>will</u> activity, backwards

Sailing in "sailing the waves" exudes a left to right and back again movement, evoking an activity in time, more permanent, eternal.

Audience

"He dropped it", a sudden movement forwards and down on dropped. 'He' is a 'hold' before releasing on 'dropped'.

This, of course, is only a drop in the ocean.

Training to become a professional eurythmist takes at least 4 years full time effort. But everyone can begin where they're at.

The benefits are legion.

IV

A few basic exercises:

- Contraction and expansion of the whole body. Forwards and back, the right and back, to the left and back, contracting a little down and backwards and expanding forwards.

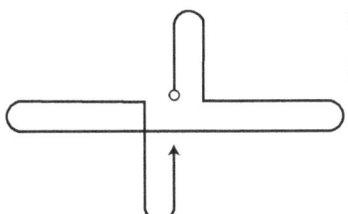 Contracting, getting small and expanding, getting gradually, through every point bigger four times.

- Spiralling in and out

   And in any direction

Play around with it!

- Five pointed star, facing front-on, the right, to the left, backwards.
  The infinite variations, infinite wakefulness begins.

- I A O

    1. Building a column from within. Up <u>and</u> down, from the region of the breastbone.
    2. Opening the straightened arms as before and leaning back, opening in A (star) on the scale of the whole body, 'leaning' into the back-space, connecting with it.

3. Transferring gently to leaning into the front space, connecting this with 2.

- Lots of quick crossing of the arms.

eeee   to wake up, focusing like our eyes.

Instagram: eurythmymark
Tik-tok: springhead
Twitter: youarethecloud.com.au
My websites: eurythmy.com.au
youarethecloud.com.au

Take this further infinitely.
Doing, becoming that larynx the important bit.
<u>Beginning to speak in both word and deed as you never thought possible.</u>

Improvising, playing, discovering like the movement for "bum".

Learning to *PLaY* as children the *NaMe* of the *GaMe*, the *AiM*. *AWaKeNiNG FeeLiNGS*.

V

Eurythmy a new <u>social element</u>.

In theatre one actor speaks to another actor.

In a eurythmy performance the actor speaks 'through' the eurythmist and the eurythmist through — a fraction before and with — the actor.

    Speech-eurythmy.

There is also tone-eurythmy. Together with one or more classically trained musicians a similar process is worked through.

    Another time!

The Social Art
I

Being told what a B is, it's movement, is one thing.
    Similarly for K, M, N etc.
But you can discover them yourself.

Take any object as it stands or place an object in the centre of a cleared space.
    Alone or with others arranged round it in a circle.

Without talking, one person might turn the object round, upside down, pick it up and walk off with it, try to eat it, demonstrate its shape with their hands.
    The list of possible actions, movements is endless.
Then the person makes a gesture or movement indicating to another that it is now their turn.
    The process is repeated.
And so on.
    After a while we start to discover, to see certain similarities in the play, in some on the movements being made.

    *L*ifting, *M*oving, e*MB*racing, *B*a*L*an*C*ing on our head, *H*anding on.

Children do this all day!

We <u>do</u> it with our 'soul' through our eyes, our invisible arms active.

Try!   M,   B,   N,   H.

    In <u>lifting</u> something we can discover the L movement, lifting and falling, by eurythmists called simply L.

In <u>letting</u> go of a handle we can see L also.

    In <u>th</u>**r**owing, TH, R, W, G.

In <u>bumping</u> into someone,   B   M   P.

    It can be **P**ainful, **W**a**K**e you u**P**.

Without talking for ten minutes we start discovering the movements we made are the movements of the sounds.

    We <u>do</u> this – there is no telling involved.

We start to live in the sounds.

    ## To arrive where we are ?

II

There was a time when the architect sculpted and painted the building as well. Then sculpture and painting become separate art forms.

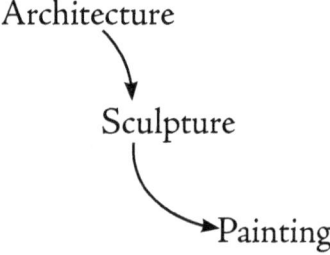

Music, arising out of singing, dance, movement, in the three came forth a plethora of instruments — folk and later classical — in countries all over the world.

Add the elements of music, e.g. short or longer notes to pictures and you get drama, poetry.

        To Sculpture,   Eurythmy.
        To Architecture,   The Social Art.

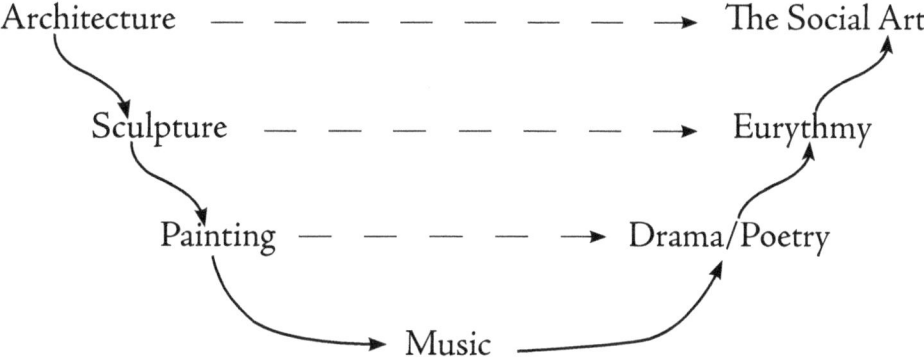

The Social Art, creating a space for all.

    And **we** all **w**ant to do that.

Angels not apes.

    Eurythmy, playing in the lines of force, runs through the whole setup.

III

And does not the ar**ch**ite**ct** (**K**, **K**), the **c**oo**k** (ba**k**er, **c**a**k**e-ma**k**er, 5**K**s), the bri**ck**layer (B, **K**) not wor**k** with the sounds?

                  Does a **n**urse not **n**urse?

    All lift.

Imagine a fa**r**me**r** without $\mathscr{R}$ ... a 'fame'; a cow that 'uminates'!

So are we just talking words or something much bigger?

If we don't have these archetypes in us can we create?
K, K, K.

Can we build, feel, love etc. etc, etc?

But with the word *Lo*$\mathcal{V}$e we have we have crossed over into the field of the $\mathcal{M}$oral.

IV

If the cow can only uminate, not **r**uminate, no milk, no butter, no cream.

And us? Will 'unning though' the day 'e of enefit'?

And a society who only 'ares' about others?

Are the moral and creative one-and-the-same?

Sounds(,)**funny**?

Hidden Script
I

The artist seeks to dis-cover what is hidden.

    Raphael, Andrei Rublev, Rembrandt, Rothko, Friedrich, Klee, Kirchner, O'Keefe.

Shakespeare.

    Beethoven.

        Musicians say he puts bums on seats.

        Why?

Bob Dylan, Jimi Hendrix.

    "And fishermen hold flowers".

Henry Lawson.

    Each succeeding great painter, great writer makes visible out of what went before, using what's in front of them for the purpose.

Something they're <u>deeply connected with</u> – lover, landscape, beautiful hall, shining wall.

    The professional eurythmist does nothing else.

A poem, play, prose-text they connect with over maybe a period of years.

    Sometimes two lines takes two weeks to get to the bottom of, dis-covering a way to express what the poet, writer <u>'captured'</u> in words – formed out of the sounds.

The activity where the inspiration came from.

The **feelings** involve**d.**
    Will.
Romanticism.
    Expressionism.
Not just art for art's sake from Paris.

II

The Social Art, not just to be pretty.
    It uses the <u>artistic process of Eurythmy</u> to uncover, strengthen the self trying to emerge —
Team, Individual, Society.
    Increasing health, creativity, morality.
Efficiency abounds.

III

Diary, poem, one word has for centuries been used to overcome pain, forthcoming execution, help us on our way.
    Now we can write with our whole body.
Making visible, strengthening the future trying to emerge.
    <u>**R**eading the **r**oom the **r**everse of 'writing' with our body as hidden script?</u>

IV

Maybe that word is "**D**etermination".
Pushing down firmly with hands and arms (especially forearms), fingers held together. As we write D –

Streaming out.

Resonating.

Drums soun**d**ing

Only **t**hese activities lead to com**m**unication, co**m**passion.

D becomes **M** ?

Lifting all up with a scooping movement and hitting with a sharp downward thrust through the arms and hands to the shoulders, the top of the head, or the waist.

The spiri**t** hi**t**s in.

- A **r**olling indication of 𝓡 with the shoulder-blades, a 'kick backwards to begin.'
- Hands, forear**m**s and pal**m**s **m**oving towards each other, arms bent at the elbow – facing each other, inner ar**m** to inner ar**m**   𝓜.
- 𝓝 touching something gently and withdrawing hand – arm/forearm going along for the ride.
- All this leads to **SH-SH**ing away like the wind shushes the leaves away. (**T** written, **SH** spoken).
- **N** again, small.

But all staying down, in the will.

Two **e**'s, arms crossed, could be added, strengthening.

> OUT OF SOME HIDDEN REALITY
> FORMING
> OUT OF THE NATURE
> OF THE SOUNDS
> WHAT WE HEAR.

Another example "**KeeP GoiNG**"

- Chopping in, **k**arate-like movement **K**.
- **P**ulling in, together, to the **p**oint of **p**ain.
- A very stro**ng**, especially with the upper arms '**g**o away', **g**et of my way, outwards movement that solidifies like nothi**ng** else on earth.

G

N right **in** makes **one G** into double **G**.

You need stro**ng** upper arms to pull a bow, aim, hold and hit the tar**g**et.
G is spoken at the back of your mouth.

In Eurythmy done especially with stro**ng** upper arms, upper le**g**s.

Or "**CoMPASSioN**"

- We write C but say **K**.
- I have 'ompassion' for others?

- Without **K** I only 'are' (not **c**are).
  - 'ontend'. (not **c**ontend)
  - am 'ind' (not **k**ind)
  - reate (not **c**reate)
- Again, **c**utting in with a **k**arate like movement I **c**an ma**k**e (not 'mae')

QUeSTioN, DouBT would be others to try out!

V

1. Consolidate it all in one word, short phrase.
2. Speak this word, phrase aloud.
3. Follow with your inner eye – see the movements.
4. Do them, as you feel it.

Examples: QR code below.

As a team the writing, whole process takes longer – all are involved.

A real referendum might be considered the Hidden Script of a country, society. Play around with all this.

<u>Do lots of **K**s to build resolve.</u>

Start to **express** what's within.

M   Discretion – living balance of thinking, feeling, willing as interaction between me and others.

S   grasping, lifting out, slowing down, seeing more exactly, understanding.

Patience.
Building this into a habit.
Scientifically sensing, becoming the <u>process</u>.

Engage
I

The Down syndrome individual comes into the room and joins with what's there.
Engages.
With words, hugs, laughter.
Warmly.
With great love.
Doesn't try to own or control.

؟ !

Not egocentric.
Peripherally centred?
Public speaking without prepared speech, teleprompter.
Future oriented.

From mental illness, toxicity, via Eurythmy, the Social Art, Hidden Script to full **expression** of what is within?

II

An art Public Speaking?

    Engaging simultaneously with both the **creative** and the **moral**.

en, in + gage, pledging yourself to the other.

    Believing in the other is something amazing waiting to emerge.

Is this not what we all need to do?

    To have as habit?

Every team?

    Every country?

    "Have I sung you a song to grow and to prosper?
    Have I sung you a song in lieu of the facts?"

III

Is not every **nail** we **knock in**, every **egg** we **beat**, every **walk** we **make public speaking**?

    Engaging?

If we haven't **come-in**, **woken-up**, we'll only *'are'* about the egg and the electric beater will send it everywhere.

    …engaging?

IV

Is not every touching of another human being in word, deed or feeling not public speaking?

    How we approach every dog, cat, lettuce leaf not public speaking?

Engaging?

Public Speaking?

V

It cannot be empathized enough that in Eurythmy our body, our being becomes a transformable larynx.

Transforming.

Echoes of the cloud?

<u>Engaging initially with the sounds leads to engaging with all things anew.</u>
    Needs are touched, **p**erceived, **e**ntered into.
The body as larynx and our other larynx speak **fr**esh thoughts, **fr**esh feelings, **fr**esh deeds.

Freely.

Common sense that was passed from generation to generation but no longer returns.

Worked-up by individuals anew.

Fragmentation

I

So en**TH**u**s**ia**s**m return**s**.

    STreaming in, in <u>resonance</u>,

In **s**eeing **e**merging in **ot**hers and us **i**ncreases   *H*. *H*appiness , wanting some-

thing to happen *W*, an e*V*ent.

    Like the twenties, **w**illful, **w**ild, *W*, *W* **y**outhful.

        I **w**ill (help).

And dri**V**e, **f**orcefulness, working to make something come **f**orth, manifest

$$I = \quad\longrightarrow\quad F \qquad F = V$$

(First only air, the second with the grunt of the throat)

vertical   two arms **f**rictioning
body   **f**orth through space, requires an impulse inwards.

         add the second part of the wa**v**e that mo**v**es **ov**er you.

Combining you get **W**A**V**e.

    Speak **U** double strength, double **U**, *w*.
Doing it with the arms brings **w**ave movements forth.

II

Here fragmentation is happening — but <u>we are in charge</u>.
    It may be that we're **taking control**.
        With fake news it is otherwise.
And all the dots that make up pictures, words on the endless screens we look at **knock us about**, out of ourselves, e**xh**a**us**t.
    (It is <u>we</u> who join-up-the-dots.)

And so much via our ears, our hearing.
    Muzak, talk unending—
Screens everywhere you look.
    A **hundred phone calls on speaker**.
Overload, explode.
    PTSD?
Fragmentation by hook or by crook?
    War?

III

Out of 'fragmented' sounds we form thoughts.
    Same sounds — different words.
    Same sounds — different thoughts.
    Same sounds — different languages.

Out of the movements of the sounds, the lines of force of the word **CALM**
    C(K)   A   L   M
    open our arms Λ => A
    we are calmed.

Do not all the dots on the screens call for the lines of force, movements to heal, re-generate, re-energize?
    And what is each sound?
eg.   F/V   force, dri**V**e.
    K/G **resolve** to **k**eep **g**oing.

ever running river, work revving us up, never tiring, robust

RoBuST.

The Sounds Have It!
I

"Casanova kissed soft lips, saw
Old worlds running off to war.
He knew, those small deeds he did
of more import than marching armies others bid;
He loved nights when clear air
quiet questions answers pair.

Christ and Casanova saw
Old worlds running off to war. They knew
that out of loving Christmas grew.
They saw stiff men of starch
stifling lovers airy arch.

Casanova kissed soft lips, held
In his hands those well-shaped hips.
Casa' never went to war,
He always wanted soft lips more."

Epic, dramatic, lyrical.

The <u>Epic</u> is about the gods (Wotan, Zeus, Apollo) and kings, emperors, heroes.

    Big, strong sounds spoken at the back of the throat.

<u>Dramatic</u> struggle of each human being on their path, totally at the teeth, strengthening.

    The teeth the toughest bones in our body.

<u>Lyrical</u>, the sounds have emerged as a force, a drama in themselves.

    How they work together to form each word.

A workplace as beautiful as the music of the sounds in the poem above?

    Becoming it's warmth!

The qualities of Love therein.

    Or the qualities of **wak**e**f**ulness and **f**un in

        "Thripsy Pillivinx,

        Inky tinky pobble boskel applesquabs? –

        Flosky! Beeble trimble flosky! – Okul

        Scratchabibblebongibo, viddle squibble tog-a-tog,

        Ferrymoyassity amsky flamsky ramsky damsky

        Cocklefeather squiggs.

            Flinkywisty pomm,

                Slushy pip."

                    (Edmund Lear)

Your team or society operating like that!

    One day, will be.

II

C

We start near the top ↻ , go down and a little up.

                              With life, lightly energetic.

Cecily, pa**c**e yourself gra**c**efully   "**C**ertainly".

            <u>Sangfroid</u>.

Running a ra**c**e one of gra**c**e!

    Carrying out a task, with ease.

Not staying heavy at the bottom of the curve but rising up a little at the end.

    Sometimes the heavy slo**g** is required.

But often it's **ang**er or **g**reed that makes us heavy.

    More gra**c**e in <u>carrying out our tasks</u>.

More lightness.

    More   **C**.

A huge block of solid iron, very heavy, with a handle on top. Go to pick it up. Strain, pull your muscles, grab hold of the handle, and "psch" — up into the air, it was light and the whole set-up takes on the movement of a set of scales.

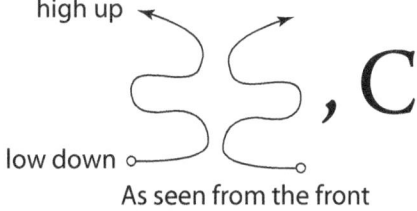

As seen from the front

Some people have it weighed-up all the time, as a habit, part of their being, making light in all they do.

    The Libran.

The road to having things weighed-up instantly, not having to ponder.

    The dancer, diplomat.

The Romans even fought wars this way.

    Centurions!

III

C is a sound common in Latin.

    In English it is often pronounced **K**.

K, as we have seen, is only air that with grunt of the throat becomes **G**.

    Go, **g**et out of my way, **g**oing, **g**ive.

C, spoken near the front of the mouth, just behind the teeth.

    G, **g**uttural, up the bac**k**.

G is like a perfect circle with an opening and a small vertical tail, anchoring.

    More standi**ng** stro**ng** and aimi**ng** that bow like William Tell — splitti**ng** the apple in two.

Gleani**ng** what needs to be done — **g**oi**ng** for it.

    To draw a perfe**c**t circle requires chan**g**i**ng** the dire**c**tion all the time, in an infinite number of tan**g**ents.

Givi**ng** everythi**ng**.

    Resolve.

100 percent.

Sticking at it.

    Never **giving**-up. (as before, **NG** = **GG**)

Hold**ing** my to**ng**ue, the future ignites.

    <u>Foresight</u>.

IV

Write   **S**

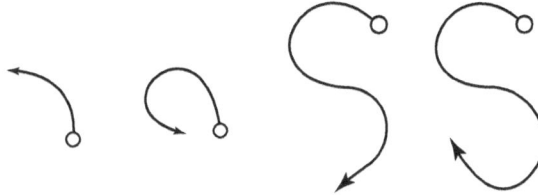

Seizing the essential, extracting (**x**=K**S**) it, slowing it down so you can really see it, so it can see/observe itself, discovering the invisible, making visible.

    Pulling yourself together.

    The **S**orcerer.

    The movement of **S** with the arms, the body is clear.

        Understanding.

    Science.

        The snake.

Mystery, history, story, **S**ophia.

    And what is science?

A slow, pain-staking proce**ss**.

    The researcher requires <u>patience</u>.

Patience.

    To di**s**cover the proce**ss** take**s** time.

The activity of writing, doing **S** slows down?

    Takes patience?

Does not every individual, every team not need patience?

    In bucket load**s**?

S with a grunt of the throat becomes **Z**.

    I am not fa**z**ed.

    A 'crazy' idea often comes after much patient effort.

    What a bu**zz**.

    Finding our way through the ma**z**e.

    Ja**zz**-walt**z**?

V

Only the tip of the iceberg, only three.

    Only inklings.

1. C   Sangfroid, weighing it up in advance, **c**arrying it out, lightness.
2. G/K   Resolve, mindin**g** one's ton**g**ue, stic**k**ing at it, seein**g** what's tryin**g** to **c**ome, foresight.
3. S/Z   Understanding, patience, dis-covering the proce**ss**, **s**izing up how to do it.

    Proce**ss**.

VI

So, we've seen how being too tied-up in our central nervous system can be overcome through the artistic process of Eurythmy, the Social Art, the Hidden Script.

The breathing freed by use of the limbs, connecting with the consonants, becoming them.

Our whole body, being involved.

Engaged.

<u>How then we come out of our imprisonment and engage.</u>

Public speaking.

And now we have got to know three of the archetypes in some detail.

What they bring. Increased

1. Sangfroid. Having it all weighed up. Ability to carry a task out.
2. Resolve. Min**ding** one's to**ng**ue. Sensi**ng** the reality tryi**ng** to emerge.
3. Patience, ability to under**s**tand. In**s**ight.

We have also seen how these archetypes, these sounds contain both moral and creative.

Without C no grace, only 'grae'.

Without K, no caring, compassion, creating no courage, no sticking at a task — only 'aring', 'ompassion', 'reating', 'ourage', etc.

Without G no hol**ding** stro**ng**, no William Tell, not bei**ng** able to **g**ive

Without S no **s**eeing, **s**ensing, **s**cience — only 'eeing', 'ening'.

But there are others:

- **W** Wanting something to happen, something meaningful.
  Devoting yourself to it.
  Devotion to what's trying to emerge.
      Setting goals? What will I?
  Deciding which services to offer.
      The forces of youth, wild twenties.

- **R** As previously written the running river carrying us along,
  Oratory,
      "Friends, Romans, countrymen,
      Lend me your ears".   (William Shakespeare)
  The cow is 24/7 worker, hard worker, doer.
      Deed.
  <u>Ability</u> to work.
      No progress without untiring work.

- **H** 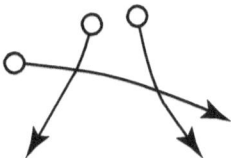 H̶ere   H̶ere   H̶ere

  Ability to act, to <u>jump-in</u>, throw yourself at the task that's before you.
      Heave twenty different cabers –   Help.
      Able to spring into action as needed.
  Napoleon!

- **F/V**   We have already felt our way in.
    Drive.
    Manifest.
    Make something for others.
    Selflessness.
    Sacrifice.

- 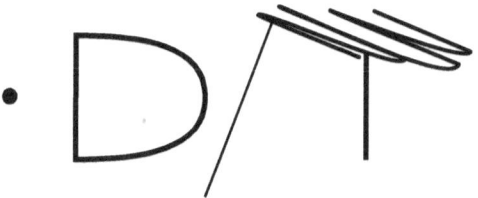   (T + grunt in the throat becomes **D**)

    Streaming out to the other with COMPASSION.
    $$(\text{th} = D/T)$$
    Resonating.
    Enthusiasm.
    Sensing worth in the other.
    'Believing' in their possibilities.
    Positivity.
        Spirit hitting in.

- **B/P**   P with grunt becomes **B**.
    Building barriers.
      Protecting.   Sobering up.   Inward, to youself:

Enables <u>seeing</u>   Seeing builds **B**?
   Calm, contained.
Pointing our what's needed, necessary.
   <u>Courtesy becoming tact of the heart</u>.
What makes the other tick…
   Their heart **pound**.

- *L*   Without looking, listening, letting unveil what the other lacks, is looking for, we cannot love.
   How often is life like locking horns on the cliff-face?
How often do we lack <u>courage</u>?
   "Dealing with reality".

A pilot must land the plane,
   The sailor stand the lifting and the falling of the sea.
Both must work with what is really there, happening.
   And if all this has been taken over by AI then all the more reason to do lots of L's… <u>courage</u>!
L   <u>courage</u>, dealing with reality released and become part of your body, your being.
   Interdependence, like rising and falling of the sea, each wave supporting, loving.
      Thinking on your feet.

Your old egocentric enthusiasms start to fade.
New ones based in reality emerge.
A <u>living</u> balance – **Majestic**

- **M**oving with what's there.
    Co**mm**unity, Co**mm**union

    M

    But **m**aintaining **m**e.

- *N*ow we can really see what's **n**eeded.
    The process is sometimes painful.
    No gain without pain.
    Doing what's **n**eeded nurtures **n**ew destiny,
        incarnates.

<u>Mag**na**nimity</u>.

L

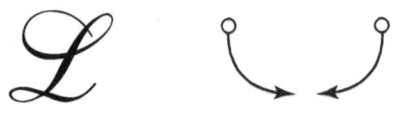

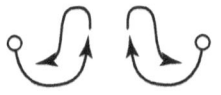 [from the front]

Lifting up and letting fall
like a bulldozer.

M

Palms and forearms moving towards each other and a little past before turning back towards each other and repeating.

Chocolate melting in the mouth.

Feel your arms strong, princely purple.

N

Gently descending down, touching momentarily before somewhat sharply but nevertheless gently withdrawing.

Snake.

[From side on]

Stretching out arms and hands, withdrawing.

VII

Three + nine makes twelve.

One of the greatest inventors and artists of modern times who — even foresaw the helicopter — did a painting the man in the middle doing "A".

Six on each side.

The gestures of the twelve consonants.

               Leonardo.

           The Last Supper.

$3^{1}/_{2}$ years of his life.

Scarborough Fair

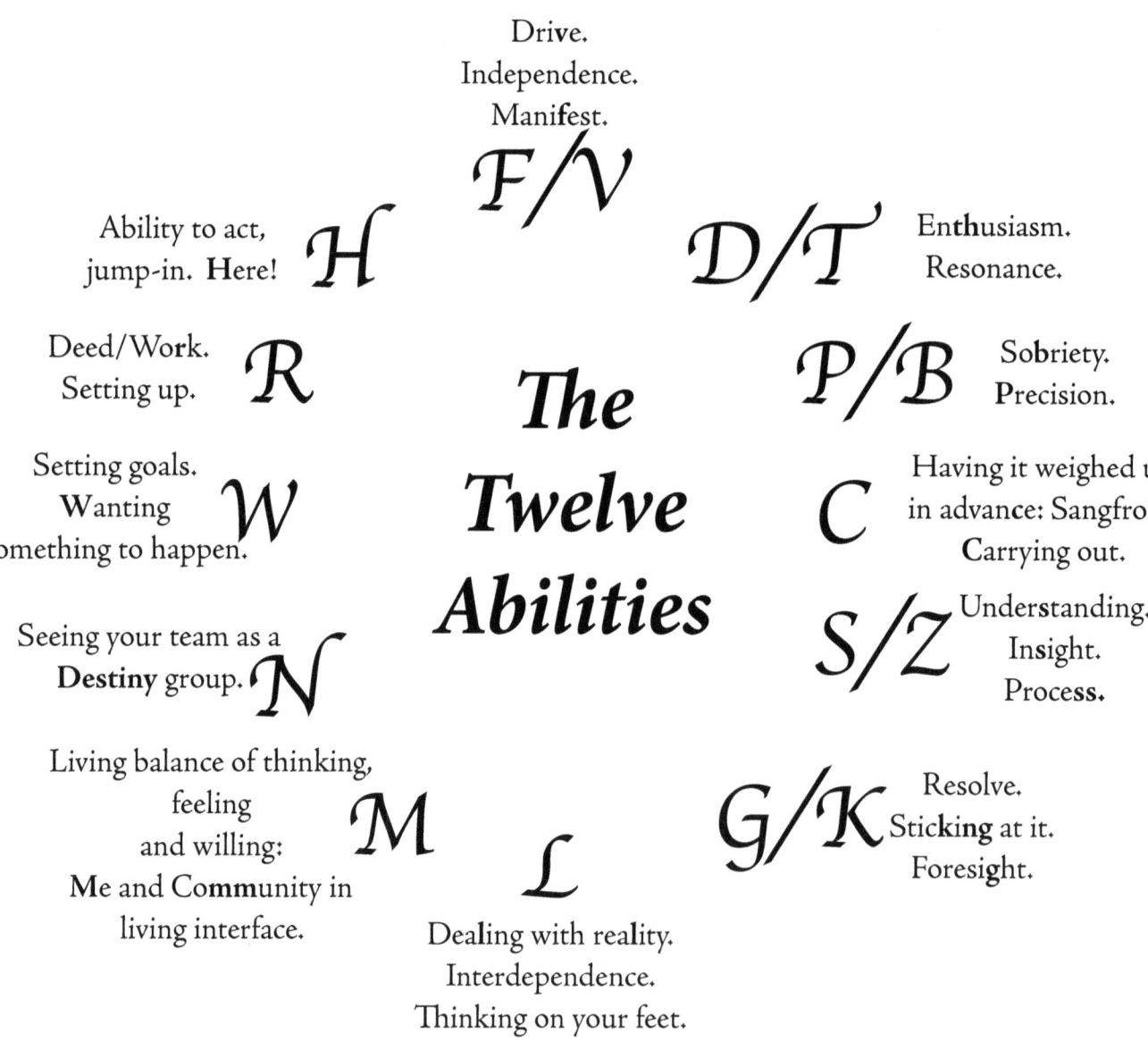

- The **SOUNDS** forming words, thoughts,

win-win   wanting something to incarnate at the depth of destiny, doubly.

Love   independence requires interdependence, $\mathcal{L}$ and $\mathcal{V}$, like

Life   real Drive arises out of Dealing with Reality.
ad infinitum —

making these sounds, movements and their forming into words a habit (Eurythmy) means

Fragmentation overcome.

- The **ABILITIES** we all need to live life, carry out our task, in the circle above work together, support each other, reinforce.

 To Weigh-things-Up you must first Sober-up from Enthusiasm, **see** what's happening.
 But without Enthusiasm, no Resolve to lift up the the rock, discovering and Dealing with Realtiy.
 No Enthusiasm, no Work.
 Wanting something to happen requires Enthusiasm.
 And only absolute Resolve leads to full Understanding.
  Their interdependence endless.

Different aspects of things in different languages but always the same sounds.

English	German	French	Russian
Tree	Baum	Arbre	Derevo
(The top of the tree coming fourth)	(The solidness of the German)	(looking at its beauty in Autumn)	(Strength)
River	Fluss	Riviére	Recca
God	Gott	Dieu	Bog

As interacting opposites to be investigated:

$$W - C$$
$$R - S/Z$$
$$H - K/G$$
$$F/V - L$$
$$T/D - M$$
$$P/B - N$$

Anything else hidden in the consonants, the abilities?

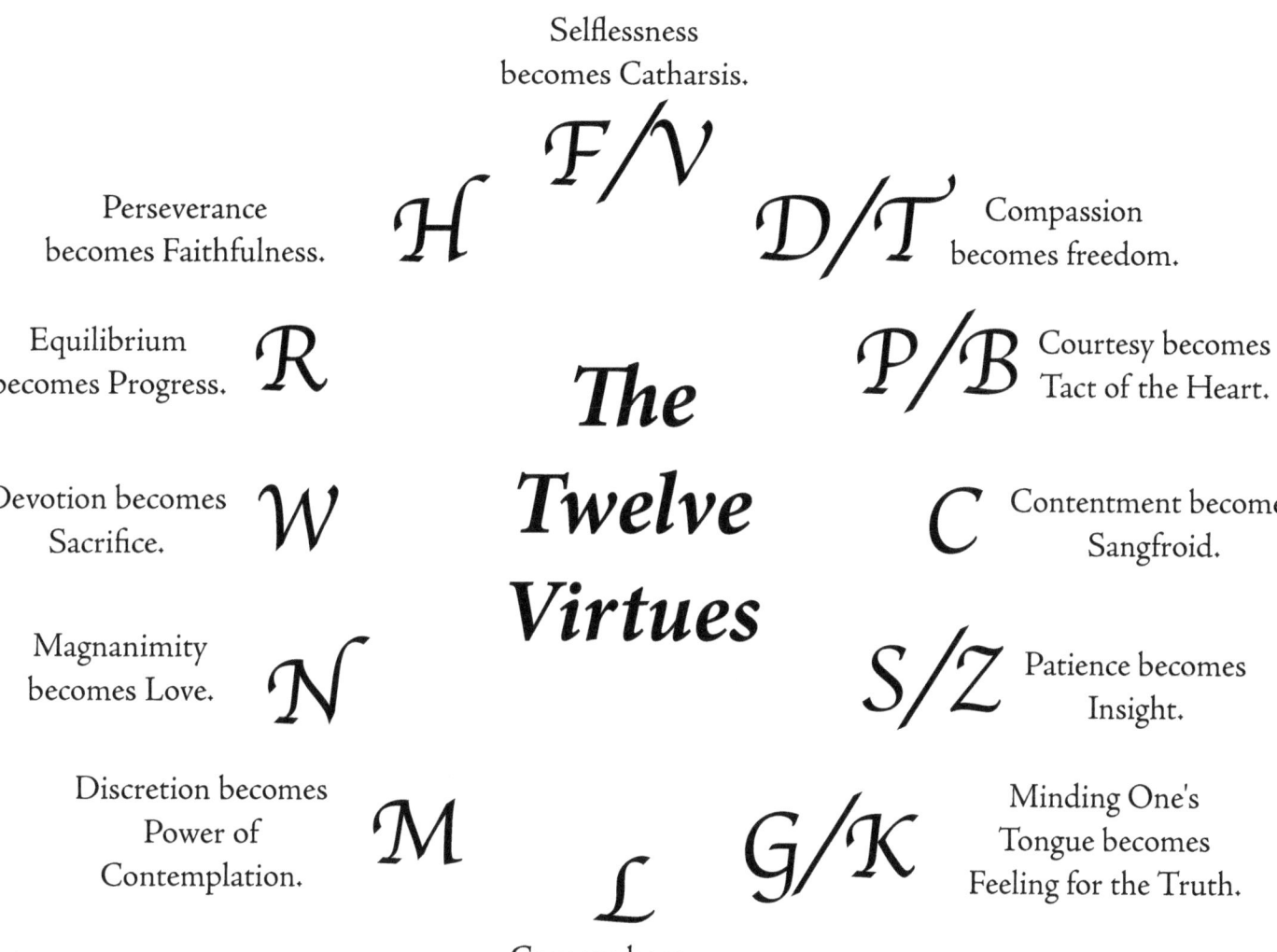

Each needs each other as well:

E.g. Compassion needs Devotion.

Courage, Minding one's Tongue.

Patience, Resolve.

Magnanimity the other eleven?

and so on.

Real Drive only through Selflessness via Dealing with Reality, *L*.

And **G**, Sticking at It/Resolve needed to Deal with Reality.

Continually *H*aving a go at the tasks to be done, Persevering.

    Devotedly   Selfless   Magnanimously

    W   *V*   *N*

WoVeN

WeaViNG.

Team, individual, society weaving new worlds.

HeRe.

Not toxic destruction.

Write them **BiG** and *FeeL* what's Happening.

*M*ove them, *PLaYinG aRouND* as you **C**an.

(Writing them with your feet incarnates you full-on
— fulfilling tasks with ease!)

Take a whole page:

Feel the continuous lifting out, extracting, slowing down, sensing.
Or **Z**, like lighting, what a bu**zz**, ja**zz**.

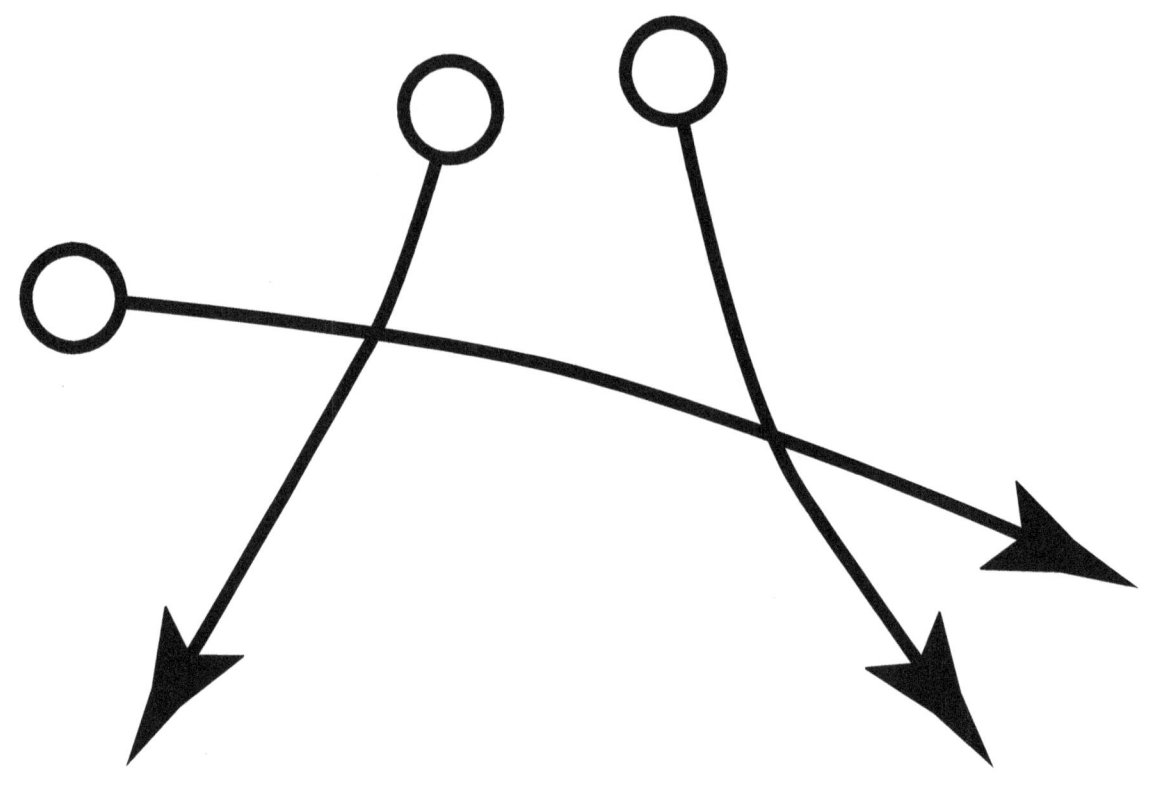

Napoleon
        <u>able</u> to jump-in,
                act.

Climbing the cliff-face, locking horns, reality's ledge clearly seen.

G

The **king** knows where its **going**.

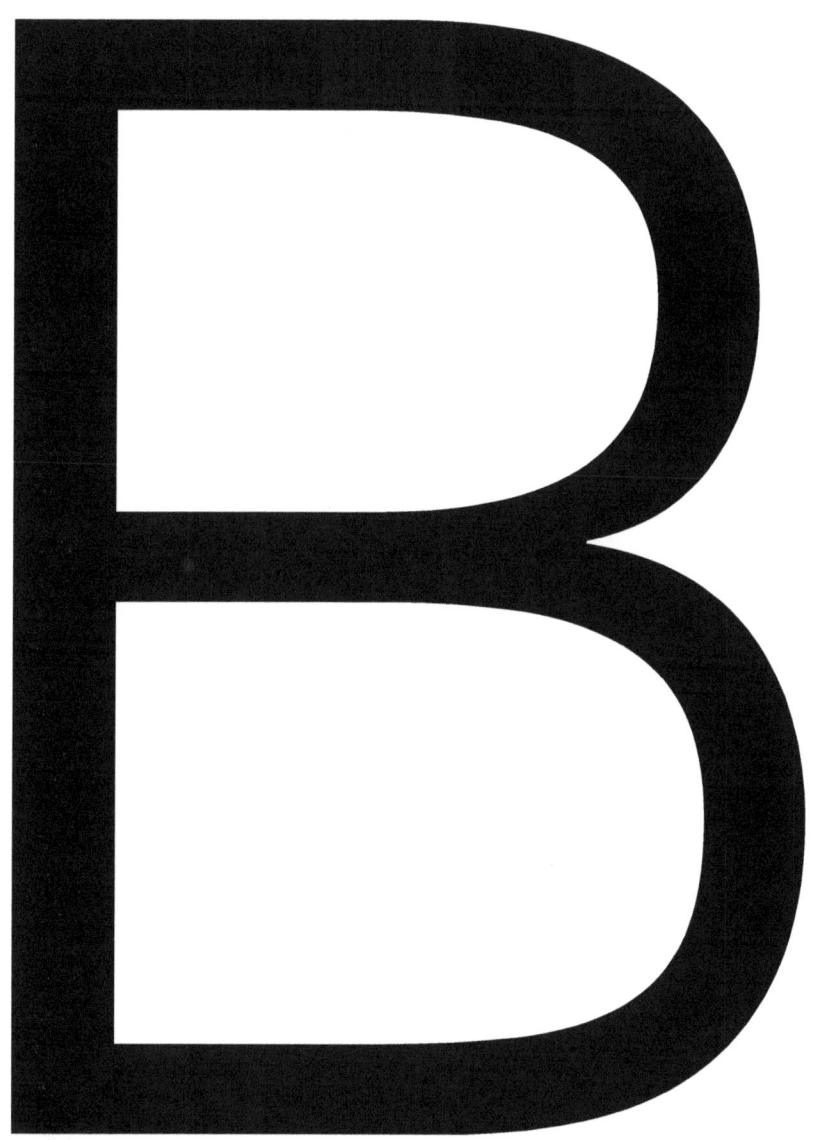

inward movement that **builds** sobriety.

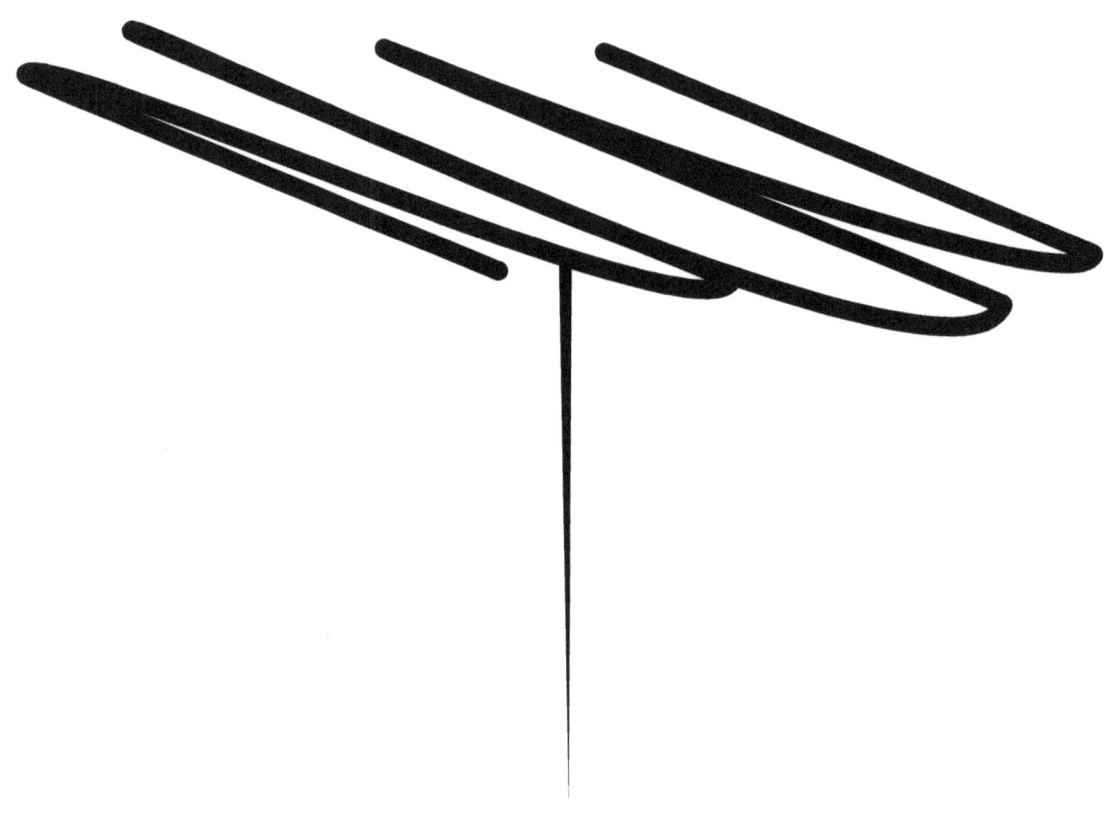

the spirit from above gathering and hitting in — like a storm in the Alps. Enthusiasm increased.

Mainly consonants in this book.

But briefly some vowels:

A   Amazed, Astounded, Aghast.
          Opening the arms to the angle we write it.
          Woarmth, Loave, Loaf.

          O+A, a diphthong as in 'for' someone.
          Or O+A, a diphthong as in 'dove'.
          O+A, moan.
          Different, flexible, English speakers can be tricky!
          A is Asking.

e   A crossing hidden therein (as in cage!).
          Bringing the arms into a crossed position actively.
          Aggressively.
          Reacting with strength to something outside.
          Strengthening.

I, i   Building a column upwards and downwards simultaneously from the region of the breastbone.
          (me, clean, seen — no clarity in English!)
          or the diphthong AI
          A going over to I.

or little i,

wit, with, big, little.

Mercury running off everywhere, fitting into too many words of contradiction — all meanings possible.

Egotistical.

To be social you must be egotistical!

No fitting in without i.

O   Embracing, encompassing from deep inside.

We say O(h) to a child who has fallen and hurt themselves.

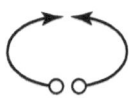 In English O is 'open':

shock, horror, orange, obvious, knowledge.

Arms opening and forming an open circle with fingers together, pointing to each other.

But in English always O + U.

Old, co(u)ld, bo(u)ld, soul   (how, enough).

An old person may have wisdom, can surround the situation, know it.

or OA, bo(a)rder, acco(a)rd, so(a)r.

or OA, moan.

Sore.

English — help! ! !

U   Arms and legs parallel – narrow.

The Twelve Senses

There is yet more to the sounds, the consonants:

- Stretching out, touching, being tender and withdrawing is **not** only **N** but also

The SeNSe of TouCH

Movement, mechanism the same.

    In both you take something with you.

Observe your tongue when enunciating **n**.

    A stop, hold at the end.

- "Mama".

The baby in the pram does **M** with its arms, legs, with its whole body, **m**embers.

    Mum's **m**ilk is healthy!

Grown-ups do the same when something tastes yummy "**mmm**".

    Tastes healthy, good.

Has life.

The SeNSe of LiFe.

My, what fun! **A**mazing, **m**agnificent, **m**agic.

    M is spoken a 'stop' that goes on, never ending.

M, the magic of **M**øvement.

             Mime   **Master.**

- And children love moving – never still.
    Lifting arms and legs when restrained.
  Adults too.
    We must need it, the sedentary lifestyle is not all:
  Walking, cycling, standing work-stations.
    Joy in feeling myself moving.
  The **SeNSe of MoVeMeNT**, your own.
    Lifting and falling like water all the time.
  Climbing hills.
    Locking horns on the cliff face like billy goats—
  Good dancers (ballet), elite athletes, all angles perceived as they manifest, in tune with the invisible unfolding.
  L & F, opposite extremes harmonizing together life, laughter …

- The fourth bodily sense the **SeNSe of BaLaNCe.**
    Children love to test their balance clambering along low brick walls.
  Ride skateboards, doing tricks.
    Archery requires balance, strength in the upper arms, upper legs to hit the target.
    Never giving up.
  Sticking at it , c(k)ome what may.
    Minding one's tongue.
  Inc(k)arnating.
  Tennis players keep low over the ball.

<u>Kee**p**ing</u> their balance at all times.

      K   The 'humour' of the c(**k**)amel in the desert.

- Individual, team, CEO must be on the **s**cent all the time — like a detective.

Soothsayer.

    Scientist.

Sensitive.

    Feeling where it'**s** going

Developing a no**s**e for a changing world.

SeNSe of SMeLL.

The brash young kid gung-ho hits winner**s**.

    But the master ha**s** learnt **patience**.

The opponent'**s** weaknesses **s**oon emerge.

    The **s**olution as to how to proceed, the proce**s**s required will emerge.

Keep searching.

    A sorcerer'**s** skill is learnt slowly.

    S, instantly insightful

Insight (as ability)

    Understanding.

- Clothes, not expensive, go well together (tasteful)—

    Bring about beauty.

Certain ……………….. certainty!

Precise.
Fitting in will with the other.
    Scales, <u>two sides together in motion</u>.
Ceding everyone their dues.
    Cecilia, Cecil,
Has it all weighed-up.
    Tastefully, with grace.
        C

The SeNSe of TaSTe.

- Sober,
    Contained.
Behind the brick fence I can see the world outside.

The SeNSe of SiGHT.

Perceiving .
    Pointing out what's <u>n</u>eeded, <u>n</u>ecessary.
P and N, opposite sides, 'becoming' each other!
    Protecting.
Papa.
    P/B

- The lion sitting astride his boulder surveying his kingdom, his domain, dominion, not doubting for a moment all the savannah is not his.

  He deems it all his, eternally.

  Don't disagree!

  His temper is great if challenged. (ch=TSH)

  Streaming out warmth like the sun.

  Warmth feeling how the other is.

SeNSe of WaRMTH.

Resonance.

Fire, enthusiasm.

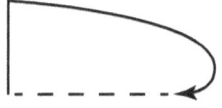
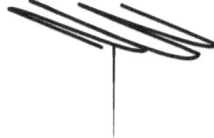

D/T

Triumphantly centred………everywhere.

Attacking at the right moment.

Giving strength, steadfast, in word and deed.

- Enthusiasm alone doesn't cut mustard.

  Drive is needed.

  The will to make something real.

  Manifest something.

  Manufacture, fabricate.

Selfless?

Promise of the paper stuff won't give lasting drive.

    Hearing the suffering of others fires us.

Giving!

    (UPRIGHT THE WAVE GOING OVER YOU).

For profit?

    For others– everyone a fellow traveller.

Hearing what they need.

    Giving.

Devoid of falseness.

    Having your finger on the pulse.

A force to reckoned with.

    Spreading out.

Via the arms, angel's wings growing back.

The ultimate motive Freedom,

        VerVe

        For eVeryone.

        (Concerto, symphony, quartet).

        Undivided seeing.

        Individuals.

Clint Eastwood, in the Bridges of Madison County:

    "I feel I've lived my whole life to spend four days with you."

L & F, 'opposites', working together.

To say such a line, sentence you **h**ave to be **h**ere, present, as **H** often is near by **H**elping.

To be here and have the wave towering over you.
Small and big.

Assessing **v**alue you must be both contained, sober and 'by' the product.
Alive.

The insurance assessor must **v**erify,
the adventurer hear danger approaching.

The **SeNSe of HeaRiNG** requires you to be present and moving in all that's around you.

Eurythmy's central exercise of
    Contraction and Expansion
becoming permanent, a habit
    always small yet big

Ensures development of the **SeNSe of HeaRiNG**.

Always present,
    The Pro**F**essional listens,
        Pro**F**icient,
        first time, e**V**erytime.

Working with the lines **of** force in his field.

Doing **F/V** requires an inward, impulse gi**V**ing mo**V**ement to be e**V**erywhere, de**V**eloping the **SeNSe of HeaRiNG**.

Every Farce, Shakespearian comedy (**Falstaff!**),
Results in rearranging the forces of destiny, of life.
JACKSON POLLOCK, LEAR'S FOOL.

ReVere.
ViViFy.
ViVid.
EVolVe.

The **SeNSe of HeaRiNG** and the sound V have the same moVement.

> You need good <u>balance</u> for <u>hearing</u>.
> A great poet has <u>movement</u> in his words, <u>sounds</u>.
> It is <u>life</u>, <u>activity in 'thinking' (thought)</u> that <u>forms</u> from the <u>sounds</u>, the words we <u>hear</u>.
> <u>Infinite materials to touch</u>, <u>infinite Egos</u>.

Touch	smell	hearing
Life	taste	word (sounds)
Movement	sight	thought, forming of
Balance	warmth	Ego, other person's
More asleep	half-conscious	need to be awake
Bodily	'soul'	spirit

In hearing you go deeper into the being of the other.
> Deeper than <u>warmth</u>, which takes you
>
> deeper than <u>sight</u>, which takes you
>
> deeper than <u>taste</u>, which takes you
>
> deeper than <u>smell</u>.

EVEN HEARING IS PUBLIC SPEAKING.

- (i) The ability to <u>see the sounds</u> being employed according to their nature, <u>their movements</u>,
- (ii) In their <u>forming thoughts</u> by
- (iii) The <u>other persons Ego, Self</u>

> gives, respectively

- (i.) The Sense of Word (Sounds),
- (ii.) The Sense of Thought,
- (iii.) The Sense of Other's Ego/Self.

Doing Eurythmy builds the twelve senses, gets them working together, the fragmented sounds working together in the building of the body as larynx.

EGO DEVELOPMENT

> Living interplay.

Not enunciating already, previously formed now dead conglomerations. This is not thinking. A 'painter' who paints like this paints like previous masters.

> Boring.
>
> We go to sleep.

II

In the artistic process of Eurythmy working in both directions is developed:

I. From hearing, via words (sounds), forming activity (thinking) to Self of the Other, and

II. Out of <u>yourself</u> <u>forming</u> <u>through use of the sounds</u> <u>what you say</u>.

        Public Speaking.
        In <u>deed</u> also.
        Ability to ENGAGE.
Common Sense, no longer common, morphs into
        Individual Sensing.

        Common Sense dead.

        <u>Individual Sensing begun.</u>

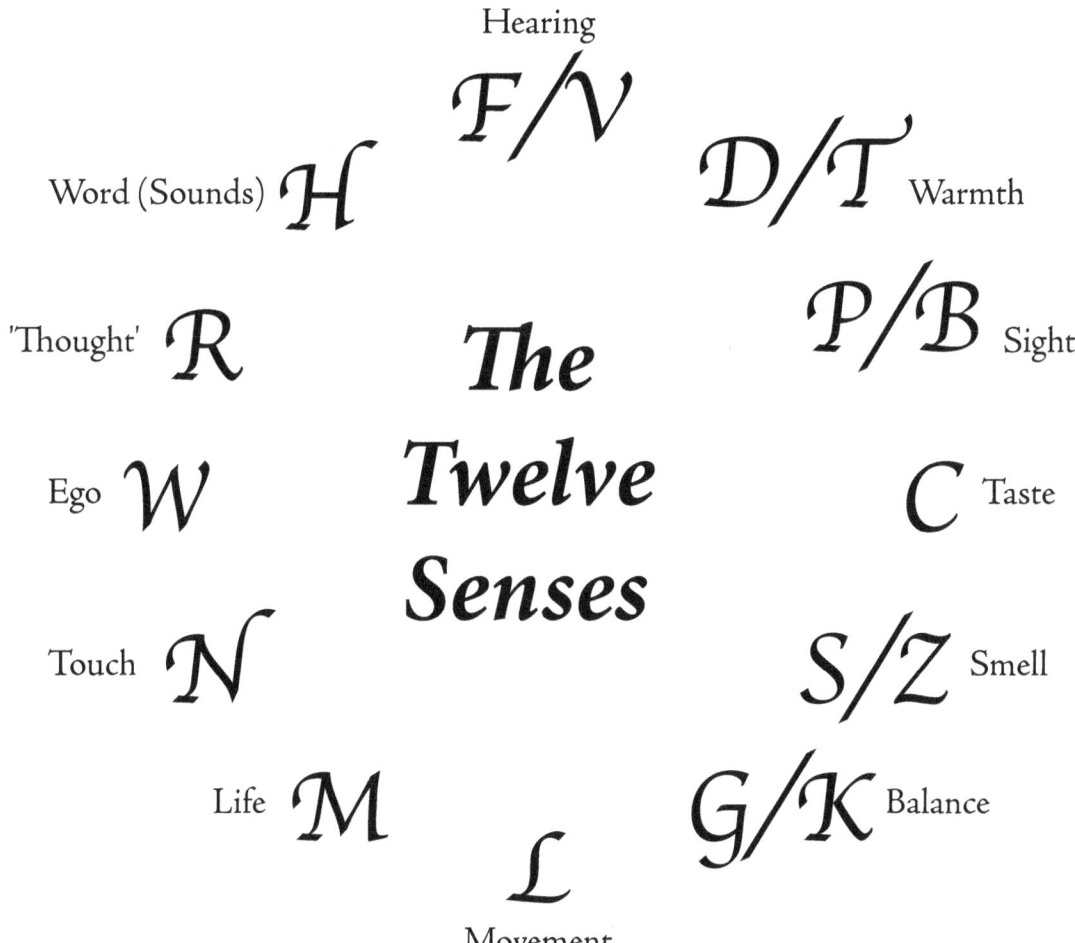

Each needs the other eleven also?
      <u>Lots of your own movement</u> leads to <u>living in the sounds</u>.
<u>T</u><u>ouching different materials</u>, <u>Egos</u>.
      <u>Hearing</u> the other requires <u>warmth</u>.
Sensing the <u>life</u> in something, <u>movement</u> in you?
      You have to <u>see</u> the <u>sounds</u> <u>forming</u>.
Is <u>smell</u> just a 'physical' affair?
      <u>Balance</u> attained through much <u>movement</u>?

No 'sensing' without the movements of the consonants become habits.

New valuing, living, loving,
Communication,
Efficiency.

Everyone Public Servants,
      Entrepreneurs all.

      Octopuses —
         Deadly   !

Pruning a tree or bush requires living in the lines of force of its structure
— Sensing into it;
Pruning the branches that need pruning.

Laws stop littering?

Bullets, bombs?

Reading the **r**oo**m**.

Walking in the shoes of the other.

Richard III

"A horse, a horse, my kingdom for a horse."

        Shakespeare has Richard III say these words as his last.
            (He says them twice in five lines).

Richard III, who killed the men and married their wives — even had two children murdered.

    The Hunchback.

An inner hunch?
    We all have one of those.
We all that other sought of hunch too — the hunch of where thi**ng**s are goi**ng**.
That word <u>g</u>oin<u>g</u> a<u>G</u>ain.
3 X G + 2 X G for 'things.'
5 lots of Resolve to both see and go this way.

    The **H**idden Script **h**elping.

H	jumping in, throwing yourself, **h**urling yourself at the task before you.
OA	warmly, with all your soul, 'for' someone else.
R	Deed, doing, WO**R**K — **R**ichard never shirked it!
S	leads to extracting the truth; seeing, understanding the situation.
E, e	And thus **s**eeing, **s**trengthening yourself, dying but never ending.

So, at the end of his life, Richard III is saying

> I'm throw**ng** myself at it 100%, with all my mi**gh**t, all my activity sens**ng** where it is **going**.

And "**King**dom"?

> **K c**(k)utt**ng** in, **k**arate, an unvoiced **G**.
> **NG** = 2 X **G**, Lots of Resolve.
> Dom = Doi**ng** … **king**ly doi**ng**.

D   streaming in, M   a new living balance of the soul faculties thinking, feeling and will that living in the situation at hand with all his body, 'deformed', give him that other sort of hunch.

<u>He lived his Hidden Script his whole life right to the end:</u>

> "Slave, I have set my life upon a cast,
> And I will stand the hazard of the die."

>   Are also some of his last words.

Lots of S's — slowing down, extracting, his destiny.

> There is hardly a stronger human being than Richard III.

(He didn't struggle to string a sentence together).

> The **g**ift of the **g**ab like perhaps no-one else.

He eNGaGeD.

100%

He lived in the sounds with his whole being, whole body to an extent hardly seen even in Shakespeare.

    Fragmented more than others.

    In the fragmentation <u>forming</u> more too.

    From Self, forming his words according to the movements of the sounds and,

        Speaking out.
        Public Speaking.
        A master.

He also says to Anne (whose father, whose husband he has just killed)
    "But 'twas thy heavenly face that set me on."

He could see her face was 'heavenly'.
    He could see 'heavenly.'
He knew it.
    An initiate?   Initiates initiate
    Initiatives.
Encyclopedias **emerge** in engaging!

Chekov Acting Method

Stanislavski's favourite actor at the Moscow Art's Theatre.

The German edition (Veit, Urachhaus, Stuttgart) restores the importance of Eurythmy omitted from the original English translation of Mikhail Chekov's in Russian written "To The Actor."

    It is little known the central part played by Eurythmy in the development of his "Psychological Gesture."

He also had it taught in his acting school at Dartington Hall, England by Australian Alice Crowther.

    Chekov practiced Eurythmy daily for years before leaving Russia.

Eurythmy, he perceived, is the road to making the phycological gesture a habit,

AN ABILITY ADVANTAGIOUS IN ALL WALKS OF LIFE.

    Students of Chekov included
        Ingrid Bergman,
        Yul Brynner,
        Gregory Peck,
        Marylin Monroe.

A famous Hitchcock film "Spellbound" includes two of these (Bergman, Peck) plus Chekov himself.

A list pf actors who used this method in later years begins with
    Anthony Quinn,
    Clint Eastwood,
    Jack Nicholson,
    Sir Anthony Hopkins —
    some include Johnny Depp.

Both the powerfulness of expression, aliveness and open warmth of these artists can be seen as a first step in the development of future humanity.

Chekov's 'psychological gesture' is none other than forming the sounds according to their character, the way they are used in the text.

    As an actor, public speaking.

From body as larynx to voice body alive, revealing the reality of the moment.

Two Tips

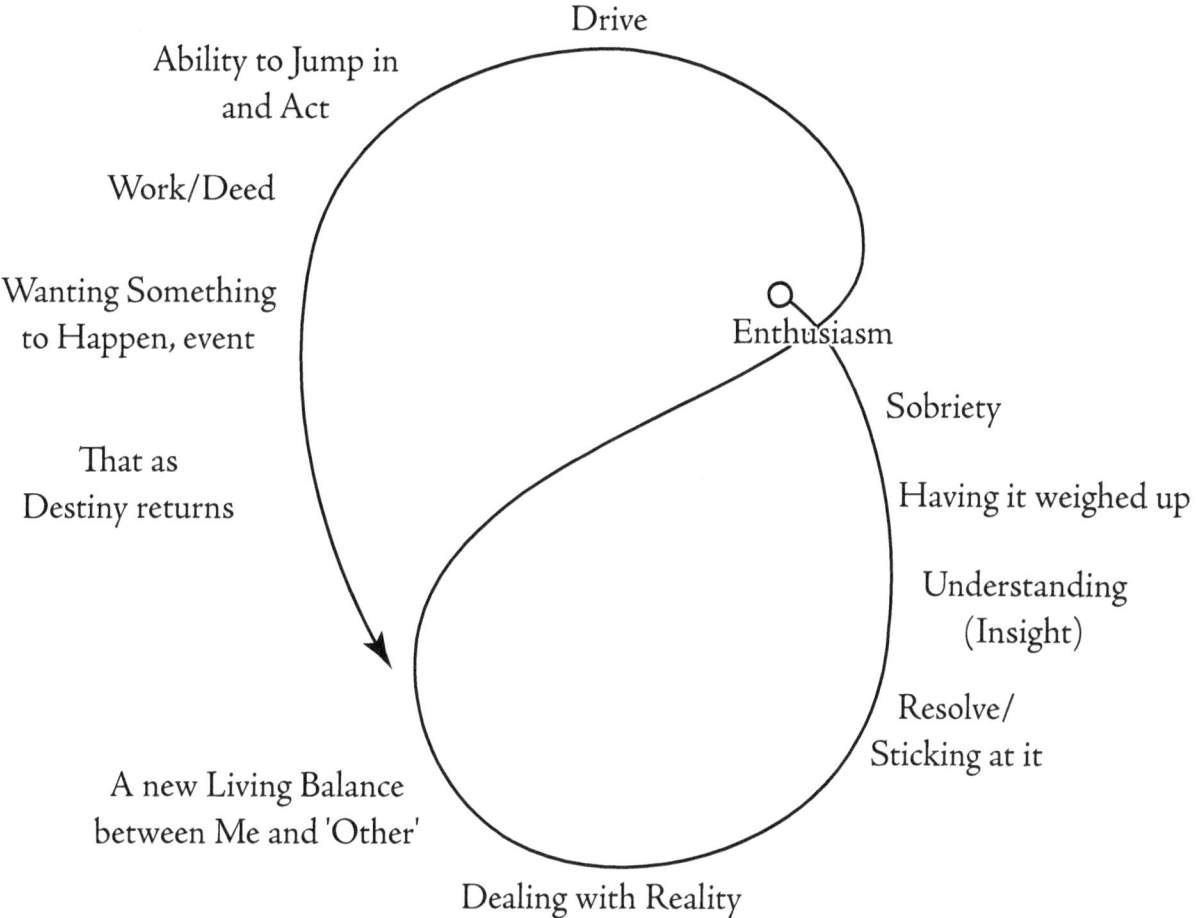

We always start with something we're enthusiastic about.
$$(TH = T = D)$$
Then to see what is in any way possible we must sober-up.
And weigh-up in advance where to cede our energy.
Patiently seeing ever more clearly where to 'attack', sting.
Going that path decisively, gregariously, never giving up.
Looking, listening, letting reality emerge.
The living balance emerging brings majesty to be enthused about.
To give us the drive arisen from the other, professionally developed, not selfish, forced, needing medication to cope.
Heralding an ability to jump in and act increased

Here I am — Helping.

Better able to work, more robust.
Happy 'cause something has happened,
What was wanted.
Destiny anew entered into.

We live in this **process** every split second, just don't notice.

II

B   M   D   N   R   L
                        G   CH   F   S   H   T

Every process begins with

Embracing,

Kissing, tasting what's there (**M**)

"Hold on": Stand-off,

No!

Stormy **r**elationship, becomes tiring.

R becomes **L**, storm clouds start to clear, lift, let in light.

I can see a**g**ain.

Take-in (German i**ch**)

Forceful,

Ma**s**ter.

Can **h**elp.

The spiri**t** enters.

<u>Live more in the process.</u>

Plus 1

- No **W**e if we're not **W**ith the others, **W**anting <u>them</u> to happen.
    No team, society, company.
  Are not customers part of the supply chain?

- No **Him** if **he**'s not <u>jumping in</u>.
    (And with <u>new living balance</u> through <u>long looking</u>.)
- Me?

*Y*ou only *Y*ou when *Y*ou do the fragmenting.

Rising and falling upright in the waves, your own movement **L** courageously dealing with reality the Capricorn in the maelstrom of business life. Manifesting **M**, becoming **F**, real drive, selflessness, the **C** Cancer's ability to make a new shell – hearing the others inner destiny **N**, touching it, magnanimously just there as the fish in the sea, **P** loving. Ego, with them, devotion — wanting that to happen, willing it **W**! the true Aries.

All becoming **M** sensing the life in me, amazing in others con-templated and met — my what kingly strength Aquarius has here. The spirit hits in compassionately resonating warmth into warmth **D**-elivering En**TH**usiasm to the worl**D**.

B-ut soBriety **B** contains, can see, and seeing contains — the courteous Virgo

<u>brought beside</u> the Painful Beating of the heart of the other.

G the whole circle of Ego development giving strength to go on never giving up, stic**K**ing at it with ever more resolve the Archer in full fli**G**ht sensing the future and shooting for it.

I'm **H**ere, I'm **H**ere, I'll **H**ave a go at this or that or **H**watever the sense of word (the many sounds) never fails me — **H**ello, I'll persevere! Gemini's help **H**werever.

Librans gra**C**efully, tastefully everything weighed up **C**eding sangfroid show.

Scorpio's the way to in**S**ight, under**S**tanding **S**ought out patient proce**SS**. The **S**corpion on the **s**cent.

Th**R**ough all this the Tau**R**us supe**R** **R**obust, **R**ea**R**ing to go **R**ea**R**ing milk f**R**om g**R**ass 24/7 — wo**R**king ha**R**d to o**R**de**R**, f**R**om the thoughts they **R**uminate. **R** giving the most activity eve**R**.

No Dreaming

Moral, morale, creative.
    All include **R**
Work –
    Hard work.
Even writing "No Dreaming" means **R**.
    The word 'writing' itself.
Word,
        Work,
        Activity
        Art
        Inner articulation
Articulated vehicle?
    Versus AI that does it all for you.

AI taking over?

    Seems like it.

Human beings obsolete?

But the drive to be moral,
>	**R**aise morale,
>	>	Be creative
>	Won't **r**etreat,
>	>	Disappear.

Often, totally depressed, we start to express ourselves through words,
>	Outbreaks of tempe**r**,

Drawings,
>	Drama (therapy).
>Words.

W	Devotion, wanting something to happen,
O (oe)	Embrace of the soul, awake/focused with e, a crossing.
R	Work, deed, hard yakka, **R**obust.
D	stream out to the other with fire, enthusiasm, resonance.
S	Being grasped, extract, exhumed, slowed down, for all to see.

Artificial Intelligence?   **Human Love!**
>	Moral, morale, creative.

ForMing.
>	FreedoM.
Taking control.

It's All About

Charm.

Charm of cobbled streets,
        Curved buildings, windows, roofs —
                mountains appearing between them.

Narrow lanes, balconies of Seville.

Even cruises a search for the charm that no longer is?
                (Cruises to the Antarctic!)

        Only greed and going broke.

'People' and companies.
Not companions.

Cutting each other's throats the only public speaking.
        The charm that was is no longer.

The friendly smile of the bar owner in Seville will only come back again if we learn to speak anew?
        Out of the sounds?

Sounds like it.

Will You?

Charm, a magic incantation or song germinating.

Charm, germ, chanson, Enchantment.

The **P**romenades of '**P**aris' **p**ublic **s**peaking!

BeLieVing

In   the   other.
FaVouring.
           (Heeding, Hearing)
ReVerence, Self-lessness, driVe not needing medication.
        Road to efficiency,
           Performance.

           Via Forming.

"A house divided cannot stand…"
        Abraham Lincoln.

"It is very kind of the Great White Chief to give us this land…"
                      Chief Seattle.

ZoRo

(ou) !

*L*ighter,

*L*aughter,

*L*ifting-up like the **Alps**,

*L*arynx.

The rhythm of a Swiss valley with its cows.

Simple Dwelling,

Building.

B

Songlines.

Bhiu …Beautiful.
In old Sanskrit roots of our language many consonants had H alongside:
Bh, Dh, Ph, Th, Gh etc.

Sagas & Myths,

Proverbs
"He wHo Hesitates is lost."

The bardish Irish tradition frightened the Romans off!

Sayings,   homilies
CHaRaDeS.

Rhyming slang:
"Just going up the apples and pears."

LIVING IN THE SOUNDS.

"Struth."

"DeaDly."

"INSaNe."

Bridges buckle, collapse
STReSS fractures

Lost, Lonely — Looking for Love
CLeaning, CLearing the souL.

Management, not 'anage'ent.

Only he who cries can create?

Crikey   (!) ...:

Veering   Vexing   Vying
(for)

"The small ferries still
Sing a song of joy,
That I can remember well,
When I was a boy:

Dancing lightly on the waves,
Cheerily they run,
May they never know no graves
Nor separation from the sun.

The small ferries still
Sing the song of a boy,
D'you think they will ever tell
The secret of their joy?"

Appreciation appreciates Appreciation?
   PRecious
   PRaise
      Raise
      Resu**RR**ection

The Fool the forces of life dealing with realit.

www.ingramcontent.com/pod-product-compliance
Lightning Source LLC
Chambersburg PA
CBHW061814290426
44110CB00026B/2867